D1091697

HALF MYSTIC PRESS

is an international, independent publishing house dedicated to the celebration of music in all of its forms. HMP publishes three to five books of prose, poetry, and experimental work per year, as well as two issues per year of *Half Mystic Journal*. For more information, books similar to this one, and submission guidelines, please visit www.halfmystic.com.

praise for knock

The incantatory poems in Melissa Atkinson Mercer's *Knock* "speak miracle and rage," insistent as daybreak or high tide. These poems are reclamation spells that celebrate and reassemble the untamed, the "witch heart," the "undarkened bell" of speech: where "mountains are the tongues of women buried for the sin of lust" and "the sea is the tongue of the woman who loved kings." As elegiac as it is visionary, this collection invokes a "matriarchal oath" to bless the darkness inside and around us.

—*Emari DiGiorgio*, author of *The Things a Body Might Become* and *Girl Torpedo*

Melissa Atkinson Mercer's *Knock* is a stunning and startling exploration of sorrow and of strength. This book is both the myth of creation and of apocalypse, of how we are built and how we are destroyed. The stakes are high in these poems: "which story will you believe", we're asked, "the one where they died / or the one where they died differently". Mercer gives us both, but in a new language, the language of dismissed goddesses hoping to find homes for their silenced tongues, and her poems refuse to choose for us. These poems sing as they disturb, they fly while they allow their speakers to drown, and they call us to make sense of a senseless world while reminding us it didn't have to be so senseless. "what use is a tongue like mine" – one need only read *Knock* to find the answer, and what a glorious and impressive answer it is.

—*Anthony Frame*, author of *Where Wind Meets Wing* and editor of *Glass Poetry Press*

The haunting and lucid speakers in Melissa Atkinson Mercer's *Knock* are at once testimonial, song and portent to the psyche's anguished interiors, "We woke in the wet black heat / to the sad song our mother knew." Mercer deftly crafts this maternal lineage with an authentic connection to all the vernaculars of language, palpably casting a light on the impediments of the mind. Mercer's incantations are arresting at every turn—as the poet confronts each threshold with an uncanny sense of observation, so pristinely rendering the dualities of our enigmatic natures, "The world was a small, dark shape & we entered it." Artful, fierce and lyrical, these poems cast a spell on the reader indelibly. This book took me hostage, released me more alive and enlightened.

—*Cynthia Atkins*, author of *In the Event of Full Disclosure*

"Before fire was ever fire ... there was just this," and these poems. Melissa Atkinson Mercer's poetry riles, rich with magic and music. With the keen eye of an imagist, the poet welcomes us into a rich and raw new perspective of a familiar world. Capturing the form of interrogation, *Knock* asks what it means to define, to be defined. What good is naming, the poet asks, when the world has no interest in a complicated answer? *Knock* integrates found text into the confessional mode, confronting depression and suicide without apology. "I lean toward the difficult," our speaker assures us. "I have something to say." Musical and elusive, she won't be silenced.

—*Stacey Balkun*, author of *Jackalope-Girl Learns to Speak* and *Lost City Museum*

FIRST PRINTING, FEBRUARY 2018
HALF MYSTIC PRESS
www.halfmystic.com

EDITED *by* DANIE SHOKOOHI
and TOPAZ WINTERS

DESIGNED *by* REBEKAH MARKILLIE
and TOPAZ WINTERS

ISBN-13: 978-1-948552-00-4
ISBN-10: 1-948552-00-0

KNOCK

Melissa Atkinson Mercer

A

Half Mystic Press

Publication

for the ones who knock

table of contents

the first cure for depression is they cut out your tongue; the second is they try to give it back

& then I had four then six I spoke apocalypse; bowls of unripened limes; a knife humming with the pelt of a fox; without protest; without knowledge of what comes

mountains are the tongues of women buried for the sin of lust; mouths studded with pearls as blue-dark as bone

mother says *hold your tongue to the left it's a girl; to the right it's hours of rain over fields of potato & black-jeweled rye; to the center it's a boy it's a boy it's a boy*

father cuts the tongues from goats before the feast; because the tongue tastes of stars & sour wind; because the tongue is the home of regret

& birds became human & their wings became tongues & they could not fly

I open jars of olives & imported salt; kiss the knob of a
door blown inward by the wind; lick a cat's vomit from
the floor; the skin from the map of a fevered man's bones

the sea is the tongue of the woman who loved kings; tore open
their guts with lemon curd & her own blood; carved them with
a knife of her teeth; drowned them in a skull of milk

& I could not keep witness & I found my tongue singing
in a pail of waste

v. to produce a noise

too emphatic,

she says, tapping her glass eye on the blackened stove. I
did not raise you demonic, demonstrative, a mirror
covered by a bright cloth. I did not raise you bloodroot. I
did not feed you apples, though you stole them from the
horses' troughs. I did not praise when I was through:
opened to stain, to dusk, to honey badgers biting the
fruit from their claws. While my own mother lived, you
could not speak at all. That was the curse we chose. &
when she died, her blood-voice was vein in you, &
sapphire. You could speak, you did speak, you speak now,
my love, speak miracle & rage.

mother, ice storm

Before fire was ever fire, she says, there was just this house, fit together like a cello. Storms grew on the black lake, cracking it like marble. We plucked out the cotton sky. We took the sugar-reeds by their throats. Made flutes of them. The hill in snow ripened to a thick fruit. Mountain lions carried their cubs deep, deep into the cedar. The world was a small, dark shape & we entered it.

grandmother was cyclopean

blind of faces, could not know me without touch. But mother wore the harder duty: sky-blind, light-over-the-sea-blind, nights-into-mornings blind. She'd come upon me in the witching black—*why do you sleep, why do you sleep*—urge me out to catch the rabbits, to pin the storms to the clotheslines, the floods to my mouth. To dig up the matriarchal bones. But I (though frantic, though bold) found only the skulls of elephants. *Darling, whoever told you we were human? Take care to take the common name, to keep the center eye silent & sessile, to keep it careful, yes, & cursed.*

love was the thing i wanted to say

The house filled up & down with water. We touched each wall—

feet made of river, scarves teeming with mud & birds.

Drowned flies in the lemon tree. It took me that long

to stop counting summers, moving overhead like the quiet pull of bats.

Green fog came up each morning, a jeweled curtain.

                          There we were,
becoming fish,

breathing dark air through our sides. There was nothing so unpleasant,

just the clear noise of the frogs waking at last, how we held

hands & pointed: all the walls turned black with eyes.

oh where to begin

but in the formidable here? Madness rose out of me like
bats. As my own father said. The witch hunts were
nascent, unheralded. Pasture brimming with flame,
bodies boiled in the river. My own father said. I had
tumors in the womb, hands that couldn't keep from
magic. It was what he called the child-bearing years, the
tongue years, fog-in-me-night-&-morning years. Oh
Lord, preserver of man & beast, who may I ask has been
tasked with my unimaginable body: to take me safe
through the harvest fields, the lines of cows, a river that
rages to the touch?

too swift,

she says, too insatiable. Don't you know these things take planning? Father was salt-skinned & whiskey; built coffins in the mustard plants, in the hard mud. Chopped boards from the porch. From my bed-wall, my exorbitant spine. Back to river, bones to fish—perfect thief, I started small—sticks of butter from the pantry, the heart of a rabbit. Yes, I took the cello as my own creature, ribbed & lunged, skeletal song. Press close, little criminal, & mark this: you have no claim to the womb, to the born body. All I have is what I stole.

if you want me to tell you

why our bodies were trees,
the first answer is the place:
how we could only go so far. The yard
sloped out from the back porch,
all the men waiting there, men our father
hired to fix the plumbing.
Flies clotted the unearthed pipes, a sound
like the kitchen's always broken bulb,
how it got dark with our elbows
in the dish-water, a little light
thrown in from the next room.
& the second is that no one came to us,
though birds flew into our arms
& were fire—all of us, the same dream—
& we woke in the wet black heat
to the sad song our mother knew—
the frightful smell of our waste carried from us.

your women should be grave,

they said, your waters should swarm after their own kind.
It was not grace, no, not gravity when I placed a ghost in
the cat's mouth to carry room from room, when I taught
her to nurture the dead. No, it was not gravid, not
kindness when I put a candle in the dead calf to show its
mother there was breath. I left her to scratch at the
harvest, the blossomed moon, light in its slightest form.
This is the matriarchal oath, the first truth my mother
gave me: bless the black mountain, the creatures that root
in the night. Bless you, baby badger. Bless your witch
heart. Bless your circadian bones.

in the room of true dreams:

the thing that followed me was eating through my walls.

I woke always in the same place: skeleton light through the window, closet packed with my mother's quilts.

The darkness in my limbs smelled of lotus candles,

the kind my mother burned all through the ice winter. We sat in the circles they made in that low brick kitchen, the world moving beyond us like a sure-footed wolf.

What is it exactly you want?

You see, I have dreamed my life & what's coming has come already—even you, with your heart like a thin-throated flower,

the small lamp of your face beside me.

hush now & heed:

before sea & sky divided, there were many fish, & they multiplied. The moon is your whale mother, lovely, & I am not. Verboten in the womb, even there, you journeyed. Like me, already like me, all burial, all mask. I wanted you to cut the ribbon clean, to sew tents from ancestral dresses, stronger than floods, than tongues. I wanted you to dream beneath the long-haired cows, to dream & not to mourn, never to martyr; not to wake them yet, the cow mothers. Not to stir their blood song, their earthen hearts, not to summon—dear one, not yet— the whole & necessary sea.

too emotional,

she says, too primordial. Don't you think I cursed when the baby's bones broke inside me? Don't you think I was sea-bent, thick with jasmine & rotted pig? Don't you think my good eye was black with another's hand, that my moon-womb was worm & wasp? Did I waste what they call the body? Is that it? A woman asks & does not tell, as my own mother warned. Did I sleep with a knife between my ribs? Was a savage saint waking in my tongue?

my own strange beast

This is how a woman becomes a mountain, becomes the
wolf curled at the town's loud heart. While we gathered

mice skeletons from the kitchen walls. While badgers in
the blood birch painted the cacophonous dawn. While we
loved clean our dear silence.

Though our mouths parted & our tongues moved. Though
each dream opened a new sea in our bones & we walked

for years in that water.
Darling, my lungs were a nest of pigs—
yours, a good & fervent rain.

she says: these are my lungs

& she holds them, blurred in her hands like fog. She says there is no marriage in heaven: not the bones to their voice, not the tongue to its journey. She draws a cello on the floor in her own blood. To teach me holy songs. But I keep to the pastures, lining up goats like pews, sewing open my throat with clocks of sapphire & gold. I will not go unmarked, unmarred, unmarried. I will not go at all. Mother, in this hallowed mountain, my tongue is turbulent with acanthus, with bloodroot, with a pig's mudded hoof. My tongue, mother, my furious tongue—

standing at dawn with my mother

The river yard smelled small & black
where we hung out scarves over the stout dirt
& foxes carried the moon
in their fur. Fish slept
for weeks under the old mill bridge.

It was a pitiless land.

Our souls paused like kites in the salt-grass & I'm sorry
but what you said about me was always
about you. I tried different versions of waking:
your breath at my shoulder making sapphires in the early
fog.

I was never so clean. I spent years arriving.

& it came—the undarkened bell of my voice—
Mother, look—

knock

& it will open: so for years I tried nothing else. I knocked at the neighbor's door when I found his pigs gasping for water in the bleached dirt. I knocked to speak my hunger. On tables, on bowls, on glass goats. I knocked on the clawfoot tub, shimmered with lavender & salt, so that I could even then be clean. In the night heat, I knocked on cedars to summon owls. On the moon for rapture. If I could be loud enough, if incessant, the door might truly open—so I taught them, the thirsty pigs, lifting their hooves to fence posts: one, two, three & again, darlings, again.

*the third cure for depression is
to close your soul & count to
ten; the fourth is to be
without time*

if snakes crawl through the lavender dark; I will name
myself a refugee; become a hallway of mourning

if the jaws of mountain lions are alive with clocks & they
circle & circle; I will shout starshine at the tragic dogs; I
will lick the doorknob & head to war

if a gazelle flickers in the white morning on a bridge
weeping with cherries; if I pull blue roses from the teeth
of a girl; a rose for each time she died in the alley of
another man's winter

if I have nothing without youth I have nothing; for years
mistaken for a child & then; I was not a child not again; if
I neither speak nor ache then where will they hurl their
rocks; this is the life I pretend I don't have

v. to gain entry

which story will you believe

the one with a thousand maidens
porcelain gowns
necklaces made from fox eyes

the one where they died
or the one where they died differently
butchered in the goat fields or did they only

enter a storm
cut their hearts from their bones

a thousand new-gilled fish in the brightest water

the first miracle
the first women to try

ii

my heart is a girl mute with fish teeth

handmade blue lace
the lid of a jewelry box

honey-light inside a fox nest inside the river's dark smell

iii

welcome to the jackknife

the committee to form a committee
the nightgown stained with the dreams of wolves

welcome to the butter cakes my mother baked in a moon
the size of an oven

the first time someone called me what I became

I shouldn't have to tell you
your story was the first fruit

the first organ they cut out

dear queen of hell

dear prehistoric child-eating saint
dear shipwrecked god

like me you have been named a brutal favor
an apocryphal flight of bees

the green rust of an open field dear woman
in someone else's myth

your bones storm & blossom

v

my oracles are lungs river stones
slippery with fish

monsters
in the wet dark wearing my mother's pearls

vi

they have made me their witching hour

for months now my body a sea
emptied of light

an electric yearning

speaking doesn't make you
freer than silence

I've been famished for the right kind of notice

a meticulous infidel a shoebox
filled with bread

vii

my wolf veins are long blue skirts blackberry
bramble a girl

       hiding scared in the trees

viii

at the kitchen sink rinsing our hearts with the deer corn

the bed catches fire twice I survive
assassination I know which life

I'm choosing
which salvation which yellow dress

I know which monster I'll become

ix

I lie down & people die
I fill the rusted tub with water & people die

I roast ears of corn in the embers & people are dying

when I hold my soul still as an orchard
when I am prone to madness to sickness of the tongue
when I dig in the black wood for rabbits
when I crawl through walls

I move & time moves too oh saint of the canticle oh
invocation oh vengeful calm

x

my pilgrim eyes are a girl breathing through gills
a wood-hewn church a forest blossomed red

salt-boards in the damp black pantry

when I say I have no one I mean desire
a mountainous fish my sea-heart

a cavern I could climb inside & stay

xi

dear puzzle piece (dear animal of the fickle light)

not for the first time tomb-cold
a cathedral of beasts

no I'm not asking for clarity

xii

my fish bones guttered into candlesticks
blue shadows a girl

in a cedar bucket drinking the stars

my whale bones are impossibly human
god the buzzard

god buried in the same earth

xiii

meet me at destruction's small task

among the star clocks
the nightmares carved from ball gowns

the fragile covet of water for now
until we know better I am your porcelain sink

your whale mirror

the choice that beguiles

xiv

my sea-born blood is a cathedral's light
                    dreamlike ferocity a snake skin

        shimmered beneath the wet leaves

xv

I say they

(I mean Russian nesting dolls)
(I mean someone who has spoken for me)

if I could leave gender out of it
if foxes stumble from their nests at night to shimmer
under a long moon
if I'm a better fish-girl than you
if you speak the right name

if I could cut out your tongue to give you mine

xvi

my fierce-gleamed womb an orchard of whole moons

the architecture of a cow's mudded knee

it's like this

you can have a saint in your village or a god
you can start your own sentence or finish mine
you can thrum wholehearted after the distant boys
you can turn your future small

as a mouse bone in a dense black wood

xvii

my jackalope mouth is ecumenical
an unforeseen obstacle a girl

licking eggs from the floor

xviii

in red fog the gourd of fable

I sleep in the horses' troughs
in the electrical thrum of rabbits

I've found the theme of my failure

the milk snakes the feral memory
I lean toward the difficult

I have something to say

badgers clawing for bee song

corpses rotting into music

dark fish-girls
sapphired with salt

deep in the sewer lines they bring me
mirrored bone

a green glass tongue that bloodies the mouth

dear want (dear landlocked ghost)

hold closed your precious eye

the fifth cure for depression is
they take the shine from the
mouth of the world, put it in
your mouth; the sixth cure is
they paint your bones with
song

v. to collide

what do you remember of before

white orchids tied to the tails of pigs; pigs tied to the
table before the feast

& after
what we devour devours us

do you have a suggestion
I speak to the emerald dark; I speak to the hour when the
beasts turn home

do you have a tenable suggestion
I live in the dark of a wall called why

& what do you know of walls
I'll tell you a truth you won't see your way past

& then
I'll dig a latrine & name it thief; I'll dig a grave & climb
inside

what name did you give your sadness

is your mother sad too

before she was a myth she was a deer
wading into mountains waist-deep in stars

& your father
my father voted for a man who tore the necks from dolls

& your brothers
& my brothers also

what of your sister
one winter we were so poor that cats licked ice from our
windows & our breath
floated before us like a language of shame

is that why you're sad
my life is a list of truths I can't speak

have you tried
this alphabet is not my alphabet

yes but have you tried
I made it to the door & kicked it closed
but the other girls were luckless

define luckless
every winter two girls buried in pieces beside the sea

define buried
before I had nowhere & now I have this

what are you doing to fix it

I tried to die & they told me to leave

did you ask for help
they said I was a beast not a psalm

did you try smiling
did you go barefoot
did you rinse chicken grease from a pile of bowls; gather stars
from beneath a bed; hold a wet cloth to the base of your neck
I waded through a narrow sea; plucked a tick from the
sole of my foot

& are you better now
I freed one & there were twenty; I broke constellations &
I found a myth

why do you say you are alone

my limbs grow cold

what happened to the boy you loved
he crawled inside my face & made it bleed; he cut out my
bones & sold them in his mother's yard

& the second
he said death lives in my tongue

& your doctor
she said I was cured

& your doctor
mostly she spoke for me

what of your friends
they knock & knock

but five minutes ago you were laughing

this body is a house & the rooms are shut

but you laughed at the store clerk's joke
imagine you have entered a life from which there is no
retreat

but you laughed when the rain cleared our eyes of sound
stormfish gather my drowning to fortress their beds

but you are laughing now
friend this room is bright—this room is a cello & the
music starts

if you're a disease what is the cause

a hundred women chained in their own grime

why
fever & jealousy

why
gunshot wound; fell from a horse in war

define war
a gathering in the head

define gathering
toads clamor in the windowless rooms; someone digs up
bodies in the night's heat & hides them beneath my bed

yes but define someone
deserters were shot on sight
pockets murmured with worms & stones

& what were they deserting these ones they shot on sight
everything that happens happens now

& what did you name your sadness

if you're a disease what is the cure

the first boy I loved was a soldier for the seventh cause;
he falsified data in a government lab; he burned it down

so what is the cure
the second was the rumor of a terrible flood & I built a
boat from cabinets & fruit crates; the roots of almond
trees rivered skyward; young goats climbing & climbing
above the water's line

so are you cured
no one I love has survived; this room is a galaxy & I am
going nowhere

define love; define survive
a horse-shaped man eats his way through my womb
I wash him in unnamed constellations
I raise him a butcher & he leaves for war

& what is your sadness now

how deep within you is the
breaking; how deep within
you is the world

I eat the toenails of a young bull; the glow of honey from a stranger's throat; I eat an hour of midnight; an hour of winter; I eat all the garments in the attic; but not the socks; I eat packages of iced cakes; I eat tombstones; I eat the joints of my two lost toes; I stop eating berries because I do not know the home of death; I stop eating altogether & name myself famine; I eat the sound of it— *fam-ine*—& name myself predator & eat again; what use is a tongue like mine; they have asked to cut it out; they have asked to give it back; I should have been dainty & in love; *darling, it happens to all of us*; or at least a proper myth; *even & maybe especially now*

where exactly are you from

the spine of a country that wanted me gone

& where are you
I am gone

& where are you
in a purple field; buried beside a saint beside the head of
a goat

& what do you find
corpse flowers

& what do you find
goats without heads

& what do you find
goats in the purple meadows; goats in my throat scraping
it raw

sight, taste, or touch
I have been summoned to the borderlands; my dress is
soft & blown open in the slightest wind

are you being dramatic
is the future an assassin; is it an infection of lungs

are you being overly dramatic
inside the future is a river
inside the river is my tongue in the shape of a door
inside the door is a wolf unlocking its jaw

& inside its jaw
darling, listen: the tongue is the shape of a door

notes

"what name did you give your sadness," "& what did you name your sadness," and *"& what is your sadness now"* are found poems, taken from the titles of work by famous female authors who committed suicide.

May Ayim: "Borderless and brazen...," "Nightsong," "Sister," "Darkness"

Charlotte Perkins Gilman: "One girl of many," "She who is to come," "The wolf at the door," "A question," "Mother to child"

Alejandra Pizarnik: "The most foreign country"

Sylvia Plath: "All the dead dears," "The colossus," "Conversation among the ruins"

Anne Sexton: "As it was written," "All my pretty ones," "The room of my life," "Love letter written in a burning building," "An obsessive combination of," "Music swims back to me," "The fury of sunsets," "More than myself," "Hurry up please it's time," "Lessons in hunger," "Just once," "I remember," "Interrogation of the man of many hearts," "Barefoot"

Alfonsina Storni: "Lighthouse in the night," "My sister"

Sara Teasdale: "Flame and shadow," "Dusk in war time," "Spring in war time," "Testament," "Oh day of fire and sun," "Red maples," "Water lilies," "The new moon," "Did you never know," "It is not a word," "I am not yours," "Since there is no escape," "Come"

Virginia Woolf: "The voyage out," "The mark on the wall," "A haunted house," "Between the acts"

"if you're a disease what is the cause" was inspired by and includes quotes from "Reasons for Admission: 1864-1889," a list compiled from the log book of the West Virginia Hospital for the Insane.

acknowledgements

A Bad Penny Review: "I say they" and "my fierce-gleamed womb an orchard of whole moons" (published as "I can't promise I'll be mother")

Burnt Pine Review: "Too swift"

Four Chambers Press: "Your women should be grave," "My own strange beast," and "If you want me to tell you" (published as "Sister myth")

Paper Nautilus: "dear queen of hell"

Pittsburgh Poetry Review: "Knock"

Storyscape Journal: "Grandmother was cyclopean"

Micro-chapbook *My Own Strange Beast* (Porkbelly Press): "My own strange beast," "If you want me to tell you" (published as "Sister myth"), "Love was the thing I wanted to say" (published as "It was the thing I wanted to say"), "In the room of true dreams," "Mother, ice storm," and "Standing at dawn with my mother"

about the author

Melissa Atkinson Mercer is the author of the full-length poetry collection *Saint of the Partial Apology* (Five Oaks Press, 2017) as well as five chapbooks. Her work has appeared, or is forthcoming, in Tinderbox Poetry Journal, Moon City Review, Zone 3, Blue Earth Review, and *A Portrait in Blues: An Anthology of Identity, Gender and Bodies*, among others. She has an MFA from West Virginia University, where she won the Russell MacDonald Creative Writing Award in Poetry. She currently works and teaches at Lees-McRae College.

CPSIA information can be obtained
at www.ICGtesting.com
Printed in the USA
LVOW10s1936130318
569703LV00018B/1252/P